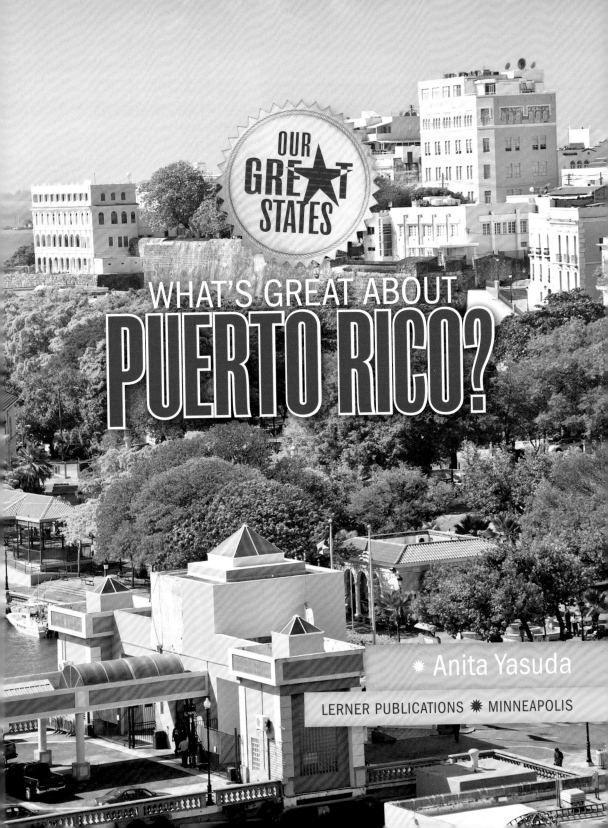

OUR GREAT STATES

WHAT'S GREAT ABOUT
PUERTO RICO?

✳ Anita Yasuda

LERNER PUBLICATIONS ✳ MINNEAPOLIS

CONTENTS

Copyright © 2015
by Lerner Publishing Group, Inc.

Content Consultant: Dr. Charles R. Venator-Santiago, Assistant Professor of Political Science, University of Connecticut

Lerner Publications Company
A division of Lerner Publishing Group, Inc.
241 First Avenue North
Minneapolis, MN 55401 USA

For reading levels and more information, look up this title at www.lernerbooks.com.

Main body text set in ITC Franklin Gothic Std Book Condensed 12/15.
Typeface provided by Adobe Systems.

Library of Congress Cataloging-in-Publication Data

Yasuda, Anita.
    What's great about Puerto Rico? / by Anita Yasuda.
        pages   cm. — (Our great states)
    Includes index.
    ISBN 978–1–4677–3872–9 (lib. bdg. : alk. paper)
    ISBN 978–1–4677–6274–8 (eBook)
    1. Puerto Rico—Juvenile literature.
I. Title.
F1958.3.Y47 2015
972.95—dc23   2014020921

Manufactured in the United States of America
1 – PC – 12/31/14

PUERTO RICO Welcomes You!

The summer never ends in Puerto Rico. This group of islands is known for sun-filled skies. Colorful fish swim in Puerto Rico's warm blue seas. And there are miles of white, sandy beaches. No wonder people think it looks like a postcard! Puerto Rico is buzzing with fun. People come here for adventures on land and sea. From its lively capital, San Juan, to smaller islands to the east, there are so many things to do! Just turn the page to find out why people love the Island of Enchantment. You will read all about the top ten things that make Puerto Rico amazing.

Mona Island

A US TERRITORY

Puerto Rico is not a state. It's a territory of the United States. That means its people are US citizens and pay taxes to the US government. But they are not represented in the US Congress. And Puerto Ricans living on the archipelago cannot vote in the presidential election.

Explore Puerto Rico's parks and all the places in between! Just turn the page to find out about the ISLAND OF ENCHANTMENT. >

Arecibo

San Juan Bay

San Juan

Bayamón

Carolina

Guaynabo

Trujillo Alto

Mayagüez

Cerro de Punta
(4,390 feet/1,338 m)

Fajardo

ATLANTIC OCEAN

Culebra Island

Caguas

El Yunque National Forest

N

Miles
0 20 40 60
0 40 80
Kilometers

CORDILLERA CENTRAL

Vieques Island

Ponce

CARIBBEAN SEA

Castillo San Felipe del Morro's walls rise 140 feet (43 meters) from the sea.

OLD SAN JUAN

> Old San Juan is the perfect place to start any trip to Puerto Rico. Walk along the Paseo de la Princesa. Take photos of the brightly painted homes, plazas, and fountains along this famous road. Be on the lookout for street performers and musicians. If you get warm, try a shaved-ice treat called a *piragua*. Enjoy your cool snack as you make your way to Pigeon Park. You can buy a bag of dried corn. Soon you'll have pigeons landing on your hands and on your head.

Next, hop on the San Juan trolley. Get off at Castillo San Felipe del Morro. There you can go on a guided tour. You will see fort workers dressed as Spanish soldiers. Ask them what life was like in the 1700s. They may even tell you a ghost story. After exploring, make your way to Castillo San Cristóbal. Walk through its old tunnels and dungeon. When you're back aboveground, stand inside a guard tower. You'll feel as if you're protecting the city!

NAMING THE TERRITORY

Spanish explorer Juan Ponce de León came to Puerto Rico in 1508. He was looking for new land and riches for Spain. As governor, he built the town of Caparra. The capital was later moved to a bay called Puerto Rico, or "Rich Port." Over time the bay became known as San Juan. *Puerto Rico* became the name for the whole archipelago.

RÍO CAMUY CAVE PARK

Keep an eye out for bats in Clara Cave! These harmless animals are most active at night.

> You cannot pass up a day trip to Camuy. These million-year-old caves are in northwestern Puerto Rico. In 1958, explorers discovered the cave system. Since then, 220 caves have been found. They are one of Puerto Rico's natural wonders. After buying your tickets, watch a short movie about the caves. Then grab a seat on the tram that will take you to the caves' entrance. From there, you can explore the caves on foot.

The first cave you'll walk through is Clara Cave. It is 170 feet (52 m) high and 695 feet (212 m) long. You'll see stalactite and stalagmite rock formations. Clara Cave opens to the Camuy River. It is the third-largest underground river in the world. Make sure to take a drink from the natural spring.

Keep exploring the caves with your guide. Who in your group will be the first to see the upside-down tree? End your day with a *piragua* in the park's picnic area. Be sure to check out the walking trails and the souvenir shop before you leave.

The tram at Río Camuy Cave Park takes you down a twisting road to a cave entrance.

TORO NEGRO STATE FOREST

> Continue your trip at Toro Negro State Forest in central Puerto Rico. Start your visit at the ranger station in Villalba. Pick up a map of the hiking trails. The forest has more than 6 miles (10 kilometers) of trails. Make your way to the popular Doña Juana Waterfall. You can cool off in the natural swimming pool below the falls.

After visiting the waterfall, stop for a quick lunch at one of the many picnic sites. Then hike La Torre trail. This uphill trail leads to a tall stone tower. It is 3,537 miles (5,692 km) above sea level. You will see the ocean and the rain forest from the tower!

There are lots of other activities near the forest. Visit Caguana Indigenous Ceremonial Park. You'll learn about the Taino Indians, who lived on the island before the Spaniards arrived. Begin your visit with a tour. Walk on the stone ball courts the Taino played on long ago. Next, look for petroglyphs carved into the rocks. Will you be able to guess what they mean?

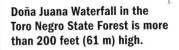

Doña Juana Waterfall in the Toro Negro State Forest is more than 200 feet (61 m) high.

A traditional Taino home

TAINO INDIANS

Explorer Christopher Columbus arrived in Puerto Rico in 1493. The island was home to the Taino Indians. Taino men fished and hunted animals such as iguanas and birds. Women grew crops such as sweet potatoes. They also picked fruits and berries. The Taino called the island *Borikén*. It meant "land of the valiant and noble lord."

11

PONCE

> Your next stop is the town of Ponce. It has the most colorful buildings in Puerto Rico. Check out the old red and black wooden firehouse in the center of the town's plaza. The building is now a museum. Make sure to pose for photos by the old fire truck.

Another popular place to visit is La Guancha Boardwalk. This boardwalk near the sea has many restaurants and shops. Try local favorites, such as fried codfish, called *bacalaitos*. Or maybe you want to try a cheese-filled turnover. As you munch on your snacks, listen to the live salsa music playing in the concert area.

After walking the boardwalk, climb El Vigia Hill. At the top is a 100-foot-tall (30 m) tower. It was built in the shape of a cross.

If you visit Ponce in February, you will see a big street fair. Carnaval has been happening every year for more than 250 years! You will hear lively music and see colorful floats. People wear masks decorated with bright designs. What will your mask look like?

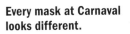
Every mask at Carnaval looks different.

PARQUE DE BOMBAS
1883

You'll have great views of Ponce and the sea from the top of the tower on El Vigia Hill.

13

ARECIBO OBSERVATORY

> If you're interested in learning more about space, you'll want to stop in Arecibo. This city is home to the Arecibo Observatory. This is a national research center. It also has one of the largest radio telescopes on Earth. The telescope is so powerful it can pick up signals from far away in space.

Learn more in the visitor center. You can look down on the telescope from the large viewing platform. The telescope is 1,000 feet (300 m) wide. Spend some time trying out the hands-on exhibits. You'll see some of the tools scientists use to study the universe. Look at photos of the inside of the observatory. Then walk through the Earth and the Solar System exhibit. You'll learn more about the planets and the sun.

After visiting the observatory, drive to the coast of Arecibo. Here you'll find the Cave of the Indian. This cave was used for Taino Indian meetings. Once inside the cave, you will see petroglyphs carved in the limestone. Make sure to get a picture of the ocean before you leave!

You can get a closer look at the telescope from the viewing platform.

See a piece of meteorite in the Arecibo Observatory visitor center.

Enjoy eating plantain chips as you cheer on players sliding into home plate at Roberto Clemente Stadium.

ROBERTO CLEMENTE STADIUM

> Puerto Rico's national sport is baseball. The island is home to several professional teams. Be sure to check out a game at Roberto Clemente Stadium in Carolina. It is smaller than stadiums on the US mainland. But you'll be sitting right next to the action. People love baseball in Puerto Rico. Some fans bring musical instruments to the games. They form bands and play between innings. Learn a new baseball chant. Join the group of kids by the team dugouts. If you're lucky, the catcher may throw a ball your way!

On your trip, you may see players from the mainland. Some like to train in Puerto Rico during the off-season. Puerto Rico has even hosted Major League Baseball games. The New York Mets and the Miami Marlins have played at Roberto Clemente Stadium. Some years, the springtime World Baseball Classic is held in San Juan. You'll see teams and players from all around the world play one another in this exciting tournament.

ROBERTO CLEMENTE

Roberto Clemente was a Puerto Rican Major League Baseball player. He won many baseball awards. He also tried hard to help people in need. Clemente did a lot of charity work. He died in a plane crash delivering goods to victims of a natural disaster. In 1973, Clemente became the first Puerto Rican and Latin American in the Baseball Hall of Fame.

RINCÓN

> There is lots of sun and sand on the west coast of Puerto Rico. Rincón is the place to visit if you want to learn to surf. It is known for big waves. Yearly surfing competitions attract world champions. Sign up for a lesson. Soon you'll be standing on your board catching waves.

Try parasailing if you are feeling bold. You'll fly high in the sky behind a boat. Invite one or two friends to join you. Look down at the water. You may spot dolphins or fish.

After a morning of fun on the water, take a walk on the boardwalk by Domes Beach. Or grab your camera and check out El Faro Lighthouse. You can climb the stairs to the top. It is 90 feet (27 m) high. The city and harbor views are fantastic! In January and February, you may be lucky enough to see a humpback whale. These months are when the whales rest and breed. You'll be able to see them from the lighthouse. As the sun sets, head back to the beach. Search for seashells in the golden sand.

Surfing (*above*) and parasailing (*below*) are just two of the activities you can enjoy in Rincón.

EL YUNQUE NATIONAL FOREST

> Put on a pair of sneakers and your swimsuit. You're going to the only tropical rain forest in the US forest system. El Yunque is in northeastern Puerto Rico. The park covers 28,000 acres (11,300 hectares) of land.

Begin your day at the visitor center. A park ranger will tell you about the birds and the mammals that inhabit the rain forest. The ranger can tell you about the Puerto Rican parrot. This bird is critically endangered. Scientists are trying to save it.

The forest is a great place to hike. There are 24 miles (39 km) of trails to choose from. As you hike, the coquí frogs will likely be singing. Try walking up Mount Britton. At the top is a tower that looks like part of an old castle. On a clear day, you will have views of the Atlantic Ocean and the Caribbean Sea. End your hike at Las Playas waterslide. It is tons of fun to slide down the stone slab into the cool water below.

SYMBOL OF PUERTO RICO

The coquí frog is a symbol of Puerto Rico. These tiny frogs are no bigger than your thumb. They may be small, but they have a big sound. The male coquí calls out loudly at night. The frog's song sounds like it is saying "Ko-kee." This is how the frog got its name. About twenty thousand coquí live in Puerto Rico.

The Puerto Rican parrot is one of the rarest birds on Earth.

CULEBRA ISLAND

> Any vacation to Puerto Rico should include a day trip to the island of Culebra. Once there, you'll find many beaches. The only way to get to the island is by plane or ferry. Be sure to buy a ticket ahead of time.

Flamenco Beach is shaped like a horseshoe. It is said to be one of the best beaches in the world. Try body boarding or kayaking in the water. Maybe you would like to explore the world under the ocean. Don't forget your snorkel gear! The island's clear, warm waters are home to coral reefs. Colorful fish and stingrays live here. Don't be surprised if a giant sea turtle swims beside you.

Back on land, build a sand castle. End your day walking through the gift shops and grabbing a bite to eat.

PUERTO RICO IN THE WAR

Puerto Rico played a key role during World War II (1939–1945). The United States built army, navy, and air force bases here. Thousands of men and machines came to the island. It became a staging area for planes and ships. Puerto Rico's location helped keep trade moving in the Caribbean Sea. Navy bases kept the Panama Canal, an important Central American waterway, safe.

You may see lots of different colored fish as you snorkel near Flamenco Beach.

MOSQUITO BAY

> One Puerto Rican stop you won't want to miss is near the island of Vieques. Water glows in the dark at Mosquito Bay. It is one of three bays in Puerto Rico that does this. Tiny organisms in the water burst into light when anything touches the water. Be sure to go on a moonless night. It will be easiest to see the water light up.

You can tour by kayak, clear canoe, or glass-bottom boat. Look up into the sky as you float through the mangroves. Because there are no city lights, the stars will be very bright. How many constellations do you see?

As you get closer to the bay, peer into the water. You'll see tiny lights everywhere! Dip your hands in the water. It's like playing with liquid glitter.

The ocean organisms at Mosquito Bay look like underwater fireworks.

YOUR TOP TEN!

Now that you've read about ten awesome things to see and do in Puerto Rico, think about what your Puerto Rico top ten list would include. If you were planning a Puerto Rican vacation, what would you like to see? Write your top ten list on a separate sheet of paper or turn your list into a booklet. You can add drawings or pictures from the Internet or magazines.

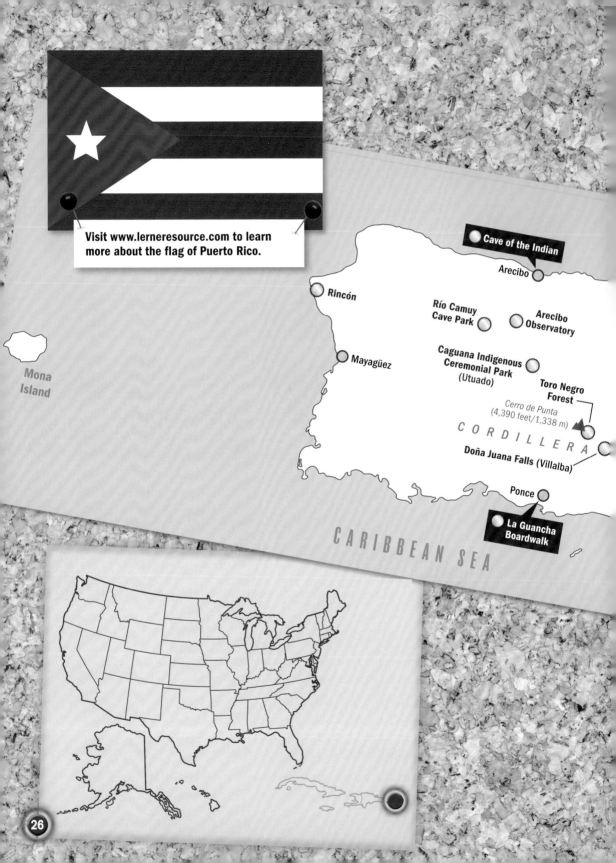

Visit www.lerneresource.com to learn
more about the flag of Puerto Rico.

Cave of the Indian

Arecibo

Rincón

Río Camuy
Cave Park

Arecibo
Observatory

Mayagüez

Caguana Indigenous
Ceremonial Park
(Utuado)

Toro Negro
Forest

Cerro de Punta
(4,390 feet/1,338 m)

C O R D I L L E R A

Doña Juana Falls (Villalba)

Ponce

**La Guancha
Boardwalk**

C A R I B B E A N   S E A

Mona
Island

PUERTO RICO BY MAP

Pigeon Park
Castillo San Felipe del Morro

Old San Juan
Castillo San Cristóbal

San Juan Bay

Bayamón

San Juan

Roberto Clemente Stadium

ATLANTIC OCEAN

Guaynabo

Carolina

Trujillo Alto

Flamenco Beach

Caguas

Mount Britton

El Yunque National Forest

Fajardo

Culebra Island

CENTRAL

N

Vieques Island

Mosquito Bay

Miles
0   20   40   60
0   40   80
Kilometers

PUERTO RICO FACTS

NICKNAME: Island of Enchantment

SONG: "La Borinqueña" by Félix Astol Artés

MOTTO: *Joannes est nomen eius*, or "John is his name"

FLOWER: Puerto Rican hibiscus

> **TREE:** kapok

BIRD: stripe-headed tanager

> **ANIMAL:** coquí

FOODS: pernil, rice, pigeon peas

CAPITAL: San Juan

AREA: 3,425 square miles (8,871 sq. km)

AVERAGE JANUARY TEMPERATURE: 74°F (23°C)

AVERAGE JULY TEMPERATURE: 81°F (27°C)

POPULATION: 3,620,897 (2013)

MAJOR CITIES AND POPULATIONS: San Juan (418,140), Bayamón (203,499), Carolina (170,404), Ponce (152,634), Caguas (86,804)

NUMBER OF US CONGRESS MEMBERS: one resident commissioner who cannot vote

NUMBER OF ELECTORAL VOTES: 0

> **NATURAL RESOURCES:** copper, nickel, oil

> **AGRICULTURAL PRODUCTS:** beef and dairy cattle, chickens, coffee, fruit, pigs

MANUFACTURED GOODS: clothing, computer and electronic products, electrical equipment, food products, medical equipment and supplies

NATIONAL HOLIDAYS OR CELEBRATIONS: Three Kings Day, Discovery Day

GLOSSARY

archipelago: a group of islands

coquí: a small tree frog found in Puerto Rico

mainland: a large area of land that forms a country and does not include islands

mangrove: a forest that grows along a coast

petroglyph: a drawing created on a rock thousands of years ago

piragua: a frozen treat made of shaved ice and covered with fruit-flavored syrup

staging area: a place where troops and machines are organized

stalactite: an icicle-like deposit hanging down in a limestone cave

stalagmite: a rock formation that grows up from the floor of a limestone cave

Taino: the native inhabitants of Puerto Rico

tram: a vehicle that runs on a track or on rails and is usually used to carry groups of people a short distance

LERNER
SOURCE

Expand learning beyond the printed book. Download free, complementary educational resources for this book from our website, www.lerneresource.com.

FURTHER INFORMATION

Anderson, Sheila. *Roberto Clemente: A Life of Generosity*. Minneapolis: Lerner Publications, 2008. Learn more about Puerto Rican baseball player Roberto Clemente, including how he helped Nicaraguan people after an earthquake.

Goldsworthy, Steve. *Puerto Rico*. New York: AV2 by Weigl, 2011. This book describes the geography, history, and symbols of Puerto Rico.

Milivojevic, JoAnn. *Puerto Rico.* Minneapolis: Lerner Publications, 2009. This book gives readers an overview of the history, geography, and culture of Puerto Rico.

A Puerto Rican Carnival
http://amhistory.si.edu/ourstory/activities/puerto
This site explains Carnaval, which is celebrated in the city of Ponce. It includes crafts, activities, and reading suggestions.

Puerto Rico Facts
http://nationfacts.net/puerto-rico-facts
Visit this site to learn more about Puerto Rico's history, geography, economy, and people.

Time for Kids: Puerto Rico
http://www.timeforkids.com/destination/puerto-rico
Explore this site to discover Puerto Rico's history, learn Taino words, and discover some of the major sightseeing attractions on the island.

INDEX

PHOTO ACKNOWLEDGMENTS

The images in this book are used with the permission of: © Ruth Peterkin/Shutterstock Images, p. 1; NASA, pp. 2–3; © MaxyM/Shutterstock Images, p. 4; © Laura Westlund/Indpendent Picture Service, pp. 4–5, 26–27; © Jason Patrick Ross/Shutterstock Images, pp. 5, 10–11, 11 (top), 20–21; © iStock/Thinkstock, pp. 6, 15 (top), 19 (top); © dp Photography/Shutterstock Images, pp. 6–7; Library of Congress, pp. 7 (LC-DIG-highsm-13647), 11 (bottom) (LC-DIG-det-4a11153), 23 (top) (HABS PR,7-SAJU,6—24); © Meaning/Shutterstock Images, p. 8; © Glyn Genin/Alamy, pp. 8–9; © Nick Hanna/Alamy, p. 9; © Amanda Kingsbury/KRT/Newscom, pp. 12–13; © Richard Ellis/Alamy, p. 13 (top); © Alberto Loyo/Shutterstock Images, p. 13 (bottom); H. Schweiker/NOAA, pp. 14–15; © Visual&Written SL/Alamy, p. 15 (bottom); © Diana Beato/Shutterstock Images, p. 16 (top); © The Rucker Archive/Icon SMI, p. 16 (bottom); © Angel Luis Garcia/El Nuevo Dia de Puerto Rico/Newscom, pp. 16–17; © George Oze/Alamy, pp. 18–19; © Emprize/Shutterstock Images, p. 19 (bottom); © Joseph/Shutterstock Images, p. 20; Tom MacKenzie, p. 21; © Lauren Orr/Shutterstock Images, pp. 22–23; © Vilainecrevette/Shutterstock Images, p. 23 (bottom); © Efrain Padro/Alamy, pp. 24–25; © John Wollwerth/Shutterstock Images, p. 25; © Bahareh Khalili Naftchali/Shutterstock Images, p. 26; © Masami Reilly/Shutterstock Images, p. 29 (top right); © Hemera Technologies/Thinkstock, p. 29 (top left); © Kotomiti Okuma/Shutterstock Images, p. 29 (bottom right); © Dmitry Kalinovsky/Shutterstock Images, p. 29 (bottom left).

Cover: © Andrew Magill/flickr.com (lighthouse); © Bryan Vincent/flickr.com (island); © Panachai Cherdchucheep/Shutterstock.com (frog); Jeff Gunn/flickr.com (town); © Laura Westlund/Independent Picture Service (map); © iStockphoto.com/fpm (seal); © iStockphoto.com/vicm (pushpins); © iStockphoto.com/benz190 (corkboard).